PRAYING
THROUGH
PAIN

Other Books by Barbara Lee

God Isn't Finished with Me Yet:
Discovering the Spiritual Graces of Later Life

Answering God's Call:
A Scripture-Based Journey for Older Adults

PRAYING THROUGH PAIN

A SCRIPTURE-BASED JOURNEY

BARBARA LEE

LOYOLAPRESS.
A JESUIT MINISTRY
Chicago

LOYOLA PRESS.
A JESUIT MINISTRY

www.loyolapress.com

Cover art credit: KavalenkavaVolha/iStock/Getty Images.

ISBN: 978-0-8294-5551-9
Library of Congress Control Number: 2022942136

Printed in the United States of America.
22 23 24 25 26 27 28 29 30 31 Versa 10 9 8 7 6 5 4 3 2 1

Contents

1

Praying with Those
Who Have Been There

There are as many kinds of pain as there are people. Serious illness, traumatic injury, or the death of someone we love can occur at any age, often without warning.

When we're sick or grieving, the ways we usually pray might not feel right. When we try to pray in our own words, the words won't come. When we try to recite prayers that we know by heart, the words don't give comfort. When an illness or injury is serious, or a loss is sudden, the impediments to prayer can include a powerful combination of negative emotions. Sometimes these feelings coalesce in a sense of having been singled out for a kind of pain that others have been spared. *Why me?*

Praying through pain very often calls for a new approach.

When our usual routine doesn't cut it, praying with Scripture is one way of bringing our feelings to prayer. The Bible is replete with stories of people who have experienced pain, fear, anger, grief, and many other emotions that can resonate with us. The people who wrote these Scriptures complained to God about being singled out or abandoned. Sitting with these stories, recognizing the emotions of Jeremiah or Paul or a psalmist, might help us understand our own feelings and listen to what God is saying to us.

The Scripture passages highlighted in this book are not exhortations to courage or endurance. Although there are many such passages in the Bible, they are unlikely to be helpful when praying through pain. No one, least of all an author of a book on prayer, knows how *you* feel. Well-meaning platitudes such as "Be patient" or "Offer it up" are no help—and may even make you feel worse. But putting yourself in the position of someone who has had similar feelings can help you find the grace in whatever you are experiencing. In other words, pray with those who have been there before us.

There is no "one size fits all" way of praying through pain. Sometimes decisions must be made, sometimes we need to discover new routines of daily prayer, and sometimes "please" and "thank you" are all we can manage. This book offers different approaches to prayer for these different situations, all drawn from the powerful tradition of Ignatian spirituality. St. Ignatius of Loyola (1491–1556), the author of the *Spiritual*

Exercises and other influential teachings on prayer and the spiritual life, taught that we should find God in all things, including our deepest feelings. Bringing those feelings—even the most negative ones—to our prayer is one approach to praying through pain.

Chapters 2 through 16 explore some of the negative emotions generated by pain through the eyes of a range of different biblical personalities, such as King David, the prophet Elijah, Paul, and Mary Magdalene. Two to three millennia ago, people felt the same helplessness that we feel and took their feelings to God in prayer.

Chapter 17 discusses the Ignatian Examen, a form of daily prayer that encourages us to identify where God has been present in our lives during the preceding day and how we have responded. For someone in serious pain, the Examen might take the place of other ways of praying, or, when possible, it can be prayed every morning or evening in addition to any other routine.

Chapter 18 offers some principles of prayerful decision making. Serious illness and major life changes often call for difficult decisions, such as where to live, what kind of assistance one needs, whether to participate in an experimental treatment, whether the suggestions of family members are helpful, and how to cope with a great many related issues. As in the chapter on the Examen, the chapter on decision making focuses on how traditional Ignatian guidelines for making prayerful decisions can apply when someone is in pain. These guidelines may also be helpful in recognizing such situations.

Chapter 19 is a compilation of very short prayers, words, or phrases that can be repeated like a mantra when anything else is too difficult—the pain is too intense, or perhaps we're being wheeled into surgery or waking in the recovery room. The mantras need no instruction; they will come to mind when they are needed.

I have used the term *pain* to encompass a broad range of possibilities: pain that is acute, such as a broken arm or migraine headache; pain that is chronic, such as rheumatoid arthritis or a slipped disc; the pain that comes with a terminal illness, such as cancer, or a temporary one, such as a severe allergic reaction or a few days harboring a particularly nasty virus. The pain that comes with the loss of someone we love may be more intense than any of these.

How to Use This Book

Don't feel obligated to read the chapters in order. Focus on the one that seems most appropriate at a particular time; a different one may resonate at another time. If you're angry or grieving or indecisive, start with the chapter that addresses your most intense feeling.

Where there is more than one Scripture passage, take one at a time. Read the passage slowly, more than once if you can.

If it's a psalm, focus on the words: What emotion was the psalmist describing? Is there one word or phrase that resonates with you? Sit with it, repeat it, and let it sink in. Why does it stand out for you? Is it drawing you closer to God?

If the Scripture is a Gospel passage or a story from the Hebrew Bible, picture the main participants: What are they seeing, hearing, doing? Many of these passages focus on one person in particular. Try to imagine that person's feelings. What grace does he or she experience? What do you want to say to God about it? What is God saying to you?

Use the "reflect" prompts after each Scripture if they are helpful; they are suggestions only. This is prayer, not study. No one can tell you what to "get out of" a passage. That is a matter of grace. It can't be forced. Savor the passage and speak directly to God in your own words about your feelings, especially the negative ones. Be open to whatever grace you may experience—whether or not it's what you expected. God is full of surprises.

God doesn't usually answer our prayers (or our questions or arguments) as clearly or directly as he spoke to some of the people whose stories are told in the Bible. Listening is an important part of all prayer, one that is essential to understanding how God speaks to each of us, here and now. Listen with your heart.

Biblical quotations are from the *New American Bible, Revised Edition* (NABR), except where otherwise specified. Quotations from the *Spiritual Exercises* of St. Ignatius of Loyola are from the Fleming translation (1996).

2

Why Me?

Someone who has been diagnosed with a terminal illness, downsized from a good job, told that her newborn has a disability, or suddenly widowed may feel singled out: my contemporaries are healthy; none of my immediate coworkers was let go; how can I care for a special-needs child, or how can I go on living? The Scripture passages in this chapter reflect the ways that ancient writers, despite their different circumstances, experienced similar emotions and prayed about them.

Lamentations 3:1–8, 21–25

I am one who has known affliction
under the rod of God's anger,
One whom he has driven and forced to walk
in darkness, not in light;
Against me alone he turns his hand—
again and again all day long.

He has worn away my flesh and my skin,
he has broken my bones;
He has besieged me all around
with poverty and hardship;
He has left me to dwell in dark places
like those long dead.
He has hemmed me in with no escape,
weighed me down with chains;
Even when I cry for help,
he stops my prayer;

But this I will call to mind;
therefore I will hope:
The LORD's acts of mercy are not exhausted,
his compassion is not spent;
They are renewed each morning—
great is your faithfulness!
The LORD is my portion, I tell myself,
therefore I will hope in him.
The LORD is good to those who trust in him,
to the one that seeks him.

The book of Lamentations is a collection of poems, probably written by the survivors of the destruction of Solomon's temple in 587 BC. The narrator of chapter 3 is described in the notes to the NABR as a "broken man"—an understatement, to say the least; a more anguished plea is difficult to find anywhere in the Bible. Yet even here, after a litany of suffering and despair that can seem like overkill, there is hope.

REFLECT

Note that the author thinks of himself as the only one so afflicted ("Against me alone he turns his hand"). In the circumstances of the destruction of the Temple, is that credible? Why or why not?

Reflect on the long list of complaints: Is it conceivable that one person could suffer all these tribulations, or is he exaggerating for literary purposes? Do you ever exaggerate your suffering? Talk to God about feeling singled out.

Psalm 139:1b–16

LORD, you have probed me, you know me:
you know when I sit and stand;
you understand my thoughts from afar.
You sift through my travels and my rest;
with all my ways you are familiar.
Even before a word is on my tongue,
LORD, you know it all.
Behind and before you encircle me
and rest your hand upon me.
Such knowledge is too wonderful for me,
far too lofty for me to reach.
Where can I go from your spirit?
From your presence, where can I flee?

If I ascend to the heavens, you are there;
if I lie down in Sheol, there you are.
If I take the wings of dawn
and dwell beyond the sea,
Even there your hand guides me,
your right hand holds me fast.
If I say, "Surely darkness shall hide me,
and night shall be my light"—
Darkness is not dark for you,
and night shines as the day.
Darkness and light are but one.
You formed my inmost being;
you knit me in my mother's womb.
I praise you, because I am wonderfully made;
wonderful are your works!
My very self you know.
My bones are not hidden from you,
When I was being made in secret,
fashioned in the depths of the earth.
Your eyes saw me unformed;
in your book all are written down;
my days were shaped, before one came to be.

The New King James Version has a more poetic translation of verse 2: "O Lord, You have searched me and known me. You know my sitting down and my rising up; you understand my thoughts from afar." This psalm, attributed to King David (139:1), is a long recitation of God's omnipresence and omniscience, extending to the minute details of the psalmist's life.

REFLECT

Ask God to rest his hand upon you. How does it feel?

Reflect on whether God's plan is "knowledge too wonderful for [you]." Ask for the grace to accept what you do not understand.

Imagine God loving you into existence before you were born. How does this affect your thinking about the purpose of your present pain?

Jeremiah 1:4–8

The word of the LORD came to me:
Before I formed you in the womb I knew you,
before you were born I dedicated you,
a prophet to the nations I appointed you.
"Ah, Lord GOD!" I said,
"I do not know how to speak. I am too young!"
But the LORD answered me,
Do not say, "I am too young."
To whomever I send you, you shall go;
whatever I command you, you shall speak.
Do not be afraid of them,
for I am with you to deliver you.

The life of a prophet in ancient Israel was a difficult one. Most were unheeded, and many were persecuted, vilified, and even killed. Jeremiah, who is believed to have belonged to a priestly family, knew all that and wanted none of it. Like Moses (Exodus 3:11, 13; 4:10), he argued that he didn't know how to speak and added that he was "too young."

Most of us are not called to prophesy, but we are all called. Someone who has lost a job may be called to do something that helps people in need. Someone who needs to move from a large house to a small apartment or assisted living may be called to evaluate all the "stuff" accumulated over time and see more clearly what really matters. And, yes, someone who has been diagnosed with a serious illness may be called to some form of suffering, as difficult as that may be to accept.

We all argue with God. Why was I one of the ones downsized? Why did I lose my spouse at such an early age? Why me?

REFLECT

Imagine your pain as a call from God, analogous to God's unwelcome call to Jeremiah. The prophet argued that he was too young. What is your argument? What is God's answer to it?

Pray with some portion of Exodus 3:1–7:7, in which Moses interposes one argument after another objecting to God's call. How did God respond each time Moses said, "But . . ."? What are your "buts"? How has God responded?

Pray the prayer of St. John Henry Newman:

God has created me to do some definite service; God has committed some work to me which has not been given to another. I have my purpose! I may never know it fully in this life, but I shall be told it in the next. I am a link in a chain, a bond of connection between persons. God has not created me for nothing! I shall do good! I shall be an instrument of peace, a preacher of truth in my own place, even when not intending it. Therefore, I will trust God. Whatever I am, wherever I am, I can never be thrown away. If I am in sickness, my sickness will serve God. If I feel I have failed, that too will serve God. If I am in confusion or sorrow, those feelings somehow serve in the Divine Plan. Nothing happens in vain. Somehow everything fits together. Even if my friends are taken away and I am thrown among strangers, if desolation makes my spirits sink and the future seems hidden from me—still, somehow, all things work together for good in God's plan of Love! Indeed, God has committed to me that work which has not been given to another. I have my purpose in this life!

Reflect on which of the individual parts of this prayer resonate with you.

Pray for the grace to trust in God's purpose when it is not apparent.

Pray for the grace to discern your purpose in life more clearly.

Jeremiah 29:11–14a

For I know well the plans I have in mind for you—oracle of the LORD—plans for your welfare and not for woe, so as to give you a future of hope.

When you call me, and come and pray to me, I will listen to you. When you look for me, you will find me. Yes, when you seek me with all your heart, I will let you find me.

Jeremiah's prophecy was directed at the Israelites who were captives in Babylon, sometime after the fall of Jerusalem in 598 BC. Yet these verses communicate comfort down through the centuries: even in times of extreme distress, we are not victims of chance or chaos; God has a plan.

REFLECT

When you call upon God in prayer, be aware that God is listening to you, but remember that this is a conversation: listen to God.

What does it mean to you to "seek [God] with all your heart"?

The Babylonian exile lasted a long time. Pray for the grace to be patient as you wait to discover God's plan for you.

Pray Thomas Merton's Prayer of Abandonment:

My Lord God, I have no idea where I am going. I do not see the road ahead of me. I cannot know for certain where it will end. Nor do I really know myself, and that I think I am following your will does not mean I am actually doing so. But I believe the desire to please you does in fact please you. And I hope I have that desire in all I am doing. I hope I will never do anything apart from that desire. And I know if I do this, you will lead me by the right road though I may know nothing about it. I will trust you always though I may seem to be lost and in the shadow of death. I will not fear, for you will never leave me to face my perils alone.

3

Impatience

It seems that every kind of illness involves waiting. We wait for an appointment (I recently waited three months to see a particular specialist, only to be referred to a different one). We wait in the doctor's aptly named waiting room; then we wait for the doctor in a chilly examination room, often clad only in a paper gown. If the doctor orders tests that can't be done in the office, we wait again for an appointment, and then we wait for the results. Sometimes we wait for our insurer to approve a medication that is not part of their formulary. Then we wait to see if it's effective.

The waiting can seem unbearable: Is that test going to be positive for a dreaded disease? At other times it is merely annoying: Has the doctor's staff forgotten I'm here? (I always bring a book to medical appointments.) The Scripture texts and reflect prompts in this chapter have been chosen for their ability to evoke some of the feelings we experience in waiting—and perhaps some of the ways that the ancient writers have found God in the experience.

Psalm 13:2–6

How long, Lord? Will you utterly forget me?
How long will you hide your face from me?
How long must I carry sorrow in my soul,
grief in my heart day after day?
How long will my enemy triumph over me?
Look upon me, answer me, Lord, my God!
Give light to my eyes lest I sleep in death,
Lest my enemy say, "I have prevailed,"
lest my foes rejoice at my downfall.
But I trust in your mercy.
Grant my heart joy in your salvation,
I will sing to the Lord,
for he has dealt bountifully with me!

The psalmist (probably King David) feels forgotten by God and has evidently been suffering a long time, as suggested by the repetition of "How long?" But at the end, the lamentation changes to trust—a frequent occurrence in the psalms.

REFLECT

Pray this psalm aloud. Which words and phrases have the most resonance with you?

Think of the psalmist's "foes" as illness, injury, or loss. Have you ever asked God "how long" you must endure pain or suffering? If so, can you follow the psalmist and rephrase it as a prayer of trust?

Who or what is your "enemy"? Illness? Pain? Impatience? Self-pity?

When or how has the Lord "dealt bountifully" with you? Give thanks.

Ecclesiastes 3:1–8

There is an appointed time for everything,
and a time for every affair under the heavens.
A time to give birth, and a time to die;
a time to plant, and a time to uproot the plant.
A time to kill, and a time to heal;
a time to tear down, and a time to build.
A time to weep, and a time to laugh;
a time to mourn, and a time to dance.
A time to scatter stones, and a time to gather them;
a time to embrace, and a time to be far from embraces.
A time to seek, and a time to lose;
a time to keep, and a time to cast away.

A time to rend, and a time to sew;
a time to be silent, and a time to speak.
A time to love, and a time to hate;
a time of war, and a time of peace.

The book of Ecclesiastes (*Qoholeth* in Hebrew, which means "collector") is an appraisal of the human condition that differs significantly from the self-assurance of other wisdom writers. The author challenges those who would claim any absolutes in this life, such as possessions, fame, success, or pleasure, all of which are subject to change and loss. The underlying theme is that God has determined the appropriate moment or "time" for each activity or experience, which is beyond human knowledge.

The book probably dates from the third century BC, when life after death was not a general belief in ancient Israel. The modern Christian, therefore, can read these lines about the transitory character of human experience with a sense of hope—of waiting for eternal life.

REFLECT

What time or season are you experiencing now? (There may be several.)

What do you need to keep? What do you need to cast away?

How do you respond to the verse that says there is a time to die?

4

Anxiety and Fear

Anxiety is the constant companion of many who suffer chronic but non-life-threatening ills, such as crippling arthritis or chronic migraine headaches. What if I fall and can't get up? Will I lose my job if I take too many sick days? Some of these concerns are legitimate and call for prayerful discernment. Others are in the category of "Don't worry; it may never happen." But when one is awake at two in the morning, conjuring all the negative possibilities, that saying doesn't help.

Fear, however, focuses on the immediate present. Someone about to have major surgery may fear not waking up after it. After a funeral, a survivor may be afraid to go home to an empty house.

The line between anxiety and fear isn't always clear. Sometimes we imagine various terrible scenarios; sometimes we are just frozen in the face of the unknown. Whatever the strength of these feelings, when we allow them to dominate, we are refusing to trust.

"Do not fear," "Do not be afraid," and similar phrases appear in the New Testament at least forty-four times—probably more, depending on the exact translation from the original Greek. Of course, if you are afraid, someone telling you "Do not be afraid" isn't much use. You will deal with your fear only if "Do not be afraid" becomes your own experience, not that of someone telling you what to do. In this chapter, you are invited to pray with stories of people who experienced anxiety and fear, and to reflect on how they found the grace in the experience.

2 Corinthians 12:7–10

Therefore, that I might not become too elated, a thorn in the flesh was given to me, an angel of Satan, to beat me, to keep me from being too elated. Three times I begged the Lord about this, that it might leave me, but he said to me, "My grace is sufficient for you, for power is made perfect in weakness." I will rather boast most gladly of my weaknesses, in order that the power of Christ may dwell with me. Therefore, I am content with weaknesses, insults, hardships, persecutions, and constraints, for the sake of Christ; for when I am weak, then I am strong.

Scholars have variously speculated that Paul's "thorn in the flesh" was a physical illness, a temptation to sin, or even a troublesome opponent in his ministry. His persistent prayer was answered not by release but by a reminder that this suffering was part of his call, a way of strengthening his ability to live it. "My grace is sufficient for you" applies to all kinds of trials. We are given the grace for whatever it is that God calls us to do here and now.

REFLECT

What is your "thorn in the flesh"? Is it physical, or is there an element of temptation, perhaps to anger or to self-pity or even failure to "beg the Lord about this"?

What are your weaknesses? How does the experience of weakness make you strong?

Ask God for the grace to trust that his grace is sufficient for you.

Pray with Matthew 26:39–44, in which Jesus "beg[s] the Lord three times" that he be spared the suffering that was about to begin. How did Jesus experience weakness? How was his "power made perfect"?

What triggers your anxiety? Review your day to identify some of the problems. Which of them call for decision making after prayerful discernment? Which of them are counter-productive?

Matthew 8:23–27

He got into a boat and his disciples followed him. Suddenly a violent storm came up on the sea, so that the boat was being swamped by waves; but he was asleep.

They came and woke him, saying, "Lord, save us! We are perishing!" He said to them, "Why are you terrified, O you of little faith?" Then he got up, rebuked the winds and the sea, and there was great calm. The men were amazed and said, "What sort of man is this, whom even the winds and the sea obey?"

REFLECT

Do you ever feel that Jesus is asleep when you need help? What do you need to do to awaken him?

Imagine being a passenger in a small boat with about a dozen other people when a sudden storm arises. Feel the sea spray and the wind on your face. See the waves churning around the side of the boat, slopping over the side. Hear your companions shouting and crying out. Is there thunder? Lightning? Can you see the shore in the distance? How do you feel?

How did the passengers feel when Jesus quieted the storm? Imagine their feeling of calm. Ask Jesus to quiet your internal storm.

Pray with Matthew 14:22–33, the story of another storm at sea, when the disciples saw Jesus walking toward them on the water during "the fourth watch of the night" (between 3 a.m. and 6 a.m.). Have you ever been awake and fearful at that time of night? Peter asked Jesus for a sign but faltered even when it was given. Does a person whose faith is strong need signs and proofs? Do you?

Psalm 27

The LORD is my light and my salvation;
whom should I fear?
The LORD is my life's refuge;
of whom should I be afraid?
When evildoers come at me
to devour my flesh,
These my enemies and foes
themselves stumble and fall.
Though an army encamp against me,
my heart does not fear;
Though war be waged against me,
even then do I trust.
One thing I ask of the LORD;
this I seek:
To dwell in the LORD's house
all the days of my life,
To gaze on the LORD's beauty,

to visit his temple.
For God will hide me in his shelter
in time of trouble,
He will conceal me in the cover of his tent;
and set me high upon a rock.
Even now my head is held high
above my enemies on every side!
I will offer in his tent
sacrifices with shouts of joy;
I will sing and chant praise to the LORD.
Hear my voice, LORD, when I call;
have mercy on me and answer me.

"Come," says my heart, "seek his face";
your face, LORD, do I seek!
Do not hide your face from me;
Do not repel your servant in anger.
You are my salvation; do not cast me off;
do not forsake me, God my savior!
Even if my father and mother forsake me,
the LORD will take me in.
LORD, show me your way;
lead me on a level path
because of my enemies.
Do not abandon me to the desire of my foes;
malicious and lying witnesses have risen against me.
I believe I shall see the LORD's goodness
in the land of the living.
Wait for the LORD, take courage;
be stouthearted, wait for the LORD!

Scripture scholars believe this psalm combines what originally were two separate sung prayers. Verses 1–6 praise the Lord and express trust in God's goodness, ending with "have mercy on me and answer me." The plea for mercy is a transition to a very different kind of prayer, begging God not to abandon the psalmist to his enemies and ending with a resolution to trust in the Lord. The shift in tone, from praise to pleading to an attempt at patience, could easily reflect the state of mind of one whose "foes" are pain and suffering.

REFLECT

Substitute "what" for "whom" in the first two verses. What do you fear?

Pray with each of the separate parts of this psalm and reflect on your feelings. Is today a day when you feel moved to praise God? Why or why not? Is today a day when you feel abandoned and need to implore God's mercy? If so, ask for the grace to "be stouthearted and wait for the Lord."

Pray with Matthew 10:28–31, in which Jesus exhorts his disciples not to be afraid "of those who kill the body but cannot kill the soul." Luke 12:22–32 expands on this theme. Imagine yourself as one of the disciples listening to this teaching. What were the disciples afraid of? How did they respond to Jesus's words? How do you respond?

5

Anger

Anger is often listed as one of the traditionally recognized stages of grief, right after denial. In the case of serious illness or major disaster, it is sometimes the first reaction. It goes much deeper than feeling singled out—*why me?* If my house is destroyed by a tornado, I am no less angry because other people in the community are going through the same experience. Of all the negative emotions that often accompany pain, anger may be the most difficult to take to our prayer—and for that reason, it's the most important to address.

Luke 15:27–29

The servant said to him, "Your brother has returned and your father has slaughtered the fattened calf because he has him back safe and sound." He became angry, and when he refused to enter the house, his father came out and pleaded with him. He said to his father in reply, "Look, all these years I served you and not once did I disobey your orders; yet you never gave me even a young goat to feast on with my friends."

The well-known parable of the prodigal son (Luke 15:11–32) is a drama with a cast of three: a wastrel younger son who repents and seeks forgiveness; his father, who responds with love and rejoicing; and a self-righteous older son, who is furious at his father's generosity. We can almost hear his outraged tone of voice: "What about me?" "Why am I left out while you give gifts to the undeserving?"

REFLECT

Put yourself in the place of the father. What do you say to the older son about his anger?

Put yourself in the place of the angry son. Is your anger justified? Why or why not?

Pray with Matthew 20:1–16, in which laborers who have worked all day are angry because of the employer's generosity toward those who have worked only an hour. Is their anger justified? Why or why not?

Jonah 4:5–11

Jonah then left the city for a place to the east of it, where he built himself a hut and waited under it in the shade, to see what would happen to the city. Then the LORD God provided a gourd plant. And when it grew up over Jonah's head, giving shade that relieved him of any discomfort, Jonah was greatly delighted with the plant. But the next morning at dawn God provided a worm that attacked the plant, so that it withered. And when the sun arose, God provided a scorching east wind; and the sun beat upon Jonah's head till he became faint. Then he wished for death, saying, "It is better for me to die than to live." But God said to Jonah, "Do you have a right to be angry over the gourd plant?" Jonah answered, "I have a right to be angry—angry enough to die." Then the LORD said, "You are concerned over the gourd plant which cost you no effort and which you did not grow; it came up in one night and in one night it perished. And should I not be concerned over the great city of Nineveh, in which there are more than a hundred and twenty thousand persons who cannot know their right hand from their left, not to mention all the animals?"

The more familiar part of Jonah's story occurs earlier: running away from God's call to preach in Nineveh, he spends three days in the belly of a large fish (some translations say a whale) and then belatedly sets out for Nineveh (Jonah 1:1–3:3). The symbolism of death and resurrection is obvious, as is the moral lesson that God's call is inescapable.

This passage shows us another aspect of Jonah's character: no longer disobedient or afraid, he is now angry, really angry, with God, "angry enough to die." He is angry because God has spared the Ninevites, even though that was the purpose of his mission. Unasked, God provides a "gourd plant"—evidently some kind of wide-leafed species tall enough to shadow Jonah's "hut"—to give Jonah shade while he nurses his anger. God unexpectedly asks him to justify his anger, but Jonah does not accept the invitation to reflection. Rather, he stubbornly persists in his selfish concern for his own comfort and refuses to relate to the Lord's concern for the repentant Ninevites.

REFLECT

Be with Jonah as he listens to God's response to his outburst ("angry enough to die"). How does it affect his anger? How would you react in his place?

What is your "gourd plant"? Are you angry with God about something that has been taken away? Imagine God rebuking you as he rebuked Jonah. How do you respond?

Numbers 11:4–8

The riffraff among them were so greedy for meat that even the Israelites lamented again, "If only we had meat for food! We remember the fish we used to eat without cost in Egypt, and the cucumbers, the melons, the leeks, the onions, and the garlic. But now we are famished; we have nothing to look forward to but this manna." Manna was like coriander seed and had the appearance of bdellium.

When they had gone about and gathered it up, the people would grind it between millstones or pound it in a mortar, then cook it in a pot and make it into loaves, with a rich creamy taste.

This event occurred "in the second year after the Israelites' departure from the land of Egypt, . . . in the wilderness of Sinai" (Numbers 1:1). It was not the first time they had complained about the food on their journey. Barely a month after their departure, in a different part of the wilderness, they "grumbled against Moses and Aaron" because of the lack of meat and bread (Exodus 16:2–3). God responded by sending quail to satisfy the people's demand for meat, and manna in place of bread (Exodus 16:4–15). The very small birds yielded a modicum of nourishment. The manna was likewise not a dish from the table of a king: coriander seeds were small and aromatic, and bdellium was a transparent, amber-colored gum resin. It's not clear who the "riffraff" among them were, or how they differed from the whole body of Israelites, but consider whether this verse can serve as a metaphor for the way a seed of anger can grow and infect a whole body.

Cucumbers and melons in the desert? An abundance of food in Egypt—where they were slaves? Where did all this anger come from? The people were given what they needed—but not what they demanded.

REFLECT

Imagine how the term *riffraff* can apply to things as well as people. Where is the *riffraff* in your feelings?

What are the "cucumbers and melons" that you long for? Why?

What is the "manna" in your life? Is it sufficient? Why or why not?

What do you want right now? What do you need?

6

Dependence

Serious illness or traumatic injury often means a loss of independence. So, too, do the diminishments that come with aging. This may be as simple as giving up driving or as life altering as needing twenty-four-hour care. At any age, a loss of independence can be humiliating and hard to accept. Our culture values—even demands—self-sufficiency. People can feel a sense of failure, as well as the indignity of role reversal, particularly when adults with a disability must be cared for by their children. When a spouse must become a caregiver, especially at an unexpectedly early age, the strains on the marriage can be severe.

Mark 2:1–12

When Jesus returned to Capernaum after some days, it became known that he was at home. Many gathered together so that there was no longer room for them, not even around the door, and he preached the word to them. They came bringing to him a paralytic carried by four men. Unable to get near Jesus because of the crowd, they opened up the roof above him. After they had broken through, they let down the mat on which the paralytic was lying. When Jesus saw their faith, he said to the paralytic, "Child, your sins are forgiven." Now some of the scribes were sitting there asking themselves, "Why does this man speak that way? He is blaspheming. Who but God alone can forgive sins?" Jesus immediately knew in his mind what they were thinking to themselves, so he said, "Why are you thinking such things in your hearts? Which is easier, to say to the paralytic, 'Your sins are forgiven,' or to say, 'Rise, pick up your mat and walk'? But that you may know that the Son of Man has authority to forgive sins on earth"—he said to the paralytic, "I say to you, rise, pick up your mat, and go home." He rose, picked up his mat at once, and went away in the sight of everyone. They were all astounded and glorified God, saying, "We have never seen anything like this."

REFLECT

When have you had to depend on others for help? How did you feel?

Can you accept help graciously when it is offered? Why or why not?

Can you ask for help when you need it? Why or why not?

John 5:1–9

After this, there was a feast of the Jews, and Jesus went up to Jerusalem. Now there is in Jerusalem at the Sheep [Gate] a pool called in Hebrew Bethesda, with five porticoes. In these lay a large number of ill, blind, lame, and crippled. One man was there who had been ill for thirty-eight years. When Jesus saw him lying there and knew that he had been ill for a long time, he said to him, "Do you want to be well?" The sick man answered him, "Sir, I have no one to put me into the pool when the water is stirred up; while I am on my way, someone else gets down there before me." Jesus said to him, "Rise, take up your mat, and walk." Immediately the man became well, took up his mat, and walked.

This enigmatic passage apparently refers to a spring that bubbled up in the pool occasionally and was believed to cure. A pool has been excavated in Jerusalem with five porticoes, which may be the one referred to in this passage. There is an ancient tradition that the water was stirred up by an angel of the Lord and that the first one to get into the pool was healed, although this theory does not seem to be accepted by modern Scripture scholars. In John's telling of the story, it is not the water of the pool that brings life; it is the word of Jesus that does so.

REFLECT

Sit with the man at the side of the pool. How has he gotten there and back all these years? Why didn't he ask someone to stay to help him into the water? Where has he gotten the patience to keep coming for thirty-eight years?

Talk to Jesus about your own problems. Is there someone you should ask for help? Pray for the grace to do so.

Patience is one of the fruits of the Holy Spirit (Galatians 5:22). Ask for it.

Romans 12:4–8

For as in one body we have many parts, and all the parts do not have the same function, so we, though many, are one body in Christ and individually parts of one another. Since we have gifts that differ according to the grace given to us, let us exercise them: if prophecy, in proportion to the faith; if ministry, in ministering; if one is a teacher, in teaching; if one exhorts, in exhortation; if one contributes, in generosity; if one is over others, with diligence; if one does acts of mercy, with cheerfulness.

The whole community of believers makes up the Body of Christ. When dependence on others for important life activities causes distress, it may help to broaden our vision: we are all interdependent; we are all connected, in Christ.

REFLECT

On whom do you depend—not only for the most obvious aspects of daily living but also for a safe environment, rapid communications, things you take for granted, large and small pleasures that contribute to your quality of life? How are you connected to each of these people?

Who depends on you? How dependable are you? Do you render help with compassion and cheerfulness?

Pray with 1 Corinthians 12:12–27, where St. Paul uses almost comical examples to drive home the interdependence of the parts of the body—if the whole body were an eye, we might see but would be unable to hear, taste, smell, or feel.

How does this metaphor help us understand our relationship to others?

John 19:25–27

Standing by the cross of Jesus were his mother and his mother's sister, Mary the wife of Clopas, and Mary of Magdala. When Jesus saw his mother and the disciple there whom he loved, he said to his mother, "Woman, behold, your son." Then he said to the disciple, "Behold, your mother." And from that hour the disciple took her into his home.

John, who is traditionally identified as "the disciple whom [Jesus] loved," tells this story as an eyewitness; the other Evangelists, who were not there, make no mention of it.

REFLECT

Imagine Mary's feelings on hearing these words. How well does she know this young disciple? How does she feel about being dependent on someone other than her son?

Mary is probably in her late forties, a relatively advanced age in the first century. What has she to look forward to? What alternatives might a middle-aged widow have today? What can families do to prepare for such an eventuality?

How do you feel about the possibility of becoming dependent? Talk to Mary about your feelings.

John is usually depicted as the youngest of the apostles. How does he feel about becoming a caregiver? How would you feel in such a situation?

Consider praying the Suscipe prayer of St. Ignatius of Loyola. This is not an easy prayer. Think of it as something to aspire to if you are not yet able to pray it wholeheartedly.

Take, Lord, and receive all my liberty, my memory, my understanding, and my entire will—all that I have and call my own. You have given it all to me. To you, Lord, I return it. Everything is yours; do with it what you will. Give me only your love and your grace. That is enough for me. (*Spiritual Exercises* 234)

A paraphrase of this prayer has been set to music by Dan Schutte. Listen to the hymn—you can find it on YouTube (https://www.youtube.com/watch?v=Mxg-qBhZ7M8). Sing it if you can.

7

Helplessness

Following a "minor" outpatient procedure, feeling weak, I slipped and fell—and I couldn't get up. It was 1:30 a.m. I felt completely helpless.

I was eventually able to reach my phone, and the night door-man came to my aid. I wasn't capable of much prayer while this was happening, except "Lord, help me!" Even after the immediate emergency had passed, it took me a while to pray about it. I was beset by all kinds of anxieties: What if I had hit my head, or broken a hip, or been unable to find the phone?

It is when we are most helpless that we realize our only help is in God.

Matthew 2:13–14

When [the Magi] had departed, behold, the angel of the Lord appeared to Joseph in a dream and said, "Rise, take the child and his mother, flee to Egypt, and stay there until I tell you. Herod is going to search for the child to destroy him." Joseph rose and took the child and his mother by night and departed for Egypt.

Is there anyone more helpless than a newborn? We don't know exactly when the Magi arrived in Bethlehem; Matthew says only "when Jesus was born." Too young to understand what was happening, he was roused from sleep in the middle of the night and jostled on the back of a donkey along a deserted, unlighted road for many hours. His parents—the only security a small baby knows—were hurried and anxious. Thus, the human experience of the Son of God began as one hunted and fleeing for his life, and in utter helplessness.

REFLECT

When have you felt helpless? Talk to Jesus about it.

Despite this dramatic episode, the infant Jesus was saved from Herod by the care of his loving parents. To whom can you turn when you feel helpless? Ask Jesus to show you.

Psalm 121

A song of ascents.
I raise my eyes toward the mountains.
From whence shall come my help?
My help comes from the LORD,
the maker of heaven and earth.
He will not allow your foot to slip;
or your guardian to sleep.
Behold, the guardian of Israel
never slumbers nor sleeps.
The LORD is your guardian;
the LORD is your shade
at your right hand.
By day the sun will not strike you,
nor the moon by night.

The LORD will guard you from all evil;
he will guard your soul.
The LORD will guard your coming and going
both now and forever.

This psalm seems to have been intended as a blessing for someone in danger, perhaps someone setting out on a treacherous journey, where he might indeed be helpless.

REFLECT

Recite this prayer aloud. From whence shall come your help?

Review the Suscipe prayer in the previous chapter.

8

Isolation

Some years ago, at a cooking class in Italy, I met a couple from Florida who had lived unhappily in New York for two years. "I hated it," the young woman told me. "You have to make an appointment to see your best friend!" She was right. People in New York City don't just drop in on friends and acquaintances. We meet for lunch or dinner in a restaurant; we get tickets to a show or a sporting event, and even when we do visit in one another's homes, it is usually after a careful comparison of calendars and obligations. The default assumption (often but not always correct) is that our friends are *busy.*

Whatever the local customs may be, a person who is sick, disabled, or otherwise in pain can't always measure up to social expectations. A new widow or widower who used to socialize with other couples is now the "extra person" at dinner parties. This can lead to a feeling of isolation.

Someone who is no longer able to attend church might feel an even deeper sense of isolation—missing the sense of community and, most of all, the Eucharist.

Can isolation be God's call, at this time and place?

The Scriptures in this chapter address that question from different points of view. Life in ancient times was communal; people were rarely alone, and there was no sense of privacy as we now understand it. Temple worship was such an integral part of life that being cut off from it was unbearable in a way that is scarcely imaginable in our pluralistic society. Solitude, however, has been understood from very early times as particularly conducive to drawing closer to God. Jesus began his public ministry with a forty-day retreat in the desert (Mark 1:12–13; Matthew 4:1–11; Luke 4:1–13). When solitude, isolation, or the feeling of being singled out for some kind of suffering is not voluntary, it can be difficult to think of it as a call to contemplation, to growth in the spiritual life. But it can become a conversion experience, if we are open to the idea that God is calling us to something new.

Luke 2:39–52

When they had fulfilled all the prescriptions of the law of the Lord, they returned to Galilee, to their own town of Nazareth. The child grew and became strong, filled with wisdom; and the favor of God was upon him. Each year his parents went to Jerusalem for the feast of Passover, and when he was twelve years old, they went up according to festival custom. After they had completed its days, as they were returning, the boy Jesus remained behind in Jerusalem, but his parents did not know it. Thinking that he was in the caravan, they journeyed for a day and looked for him among their relatives and acquaintances, but not finding him, they returned to Jerusalem to look for him. After three days they found him in the temple, sitting in the midst of the teachers, listening to them and asking them questions, and all who heard him were astounded at his understanding and his answers. When his parents saw him, they were astonished, and his mother said to him, "Son, why have you done this to us? Your father and I have been looking for you with great anxiety." And he said to them, "Why were you looking for me? Did you not know that I must be in my Father's house?" But they did not understand what he said to them. He went down with them and came to Nazareth, and was obedient to them; and his mother kept all these things in her heart. And Jesus advanced [in] wisdom and age and favor before God and man.

The period between the presentation of Jesus in the Temple (Luke 2:21–38) and the beginning of his public ministry thirty years later (Luke 3:23) is generally called "the hidden life." Jesus was isolated in the backwater town of Nazareth, obedient to his parents, and his growth in wisdom unseen except in a brief glimpse of a precocious twelve-year-old. He had thirty years in solitude to prepare for—perhaps to understand—his future role.

REFLECT

Be with Jesus as a young adult in Nazareth. Ask him how he feels about the isolation in such a place. Did he ever yearn to be among people? What are you yearning for? Talk to him about your feelings.

Where did he pray—in the small local synagogue, while working as a carpenter's apprentice, alone in the fields outside the small town? Where do you find it easiest to pray?

How did the isolation of those years prepare Jesus for his adult ministry? How can solitude prepare you to hear what God is calling you to, at this time and place?

1 Corinthians 12:4–11

There are different kinds of spiritual gifts but the same Spirit; there are different forms of service but the same Lord; there are different workings but the same God who produces all of them in everyone. To each individual the manifestation of the Spirit is given for some benefit. To one is given through the Spirit the expression of wisdom; to another the expression of knowledge according to the same Spirit; to another faith by the same Spirit; to another gifts of healing by the one Spirit; to another mighty deeds; to another prophecy; to another discernment of spirits; to another varieties of tongues; to another interpretation of tongues. But one and the same Spirit produces all of these, distributing them individually to each person as he wishes.

At the time this letter was written, Corinthian Christians were preoccupied with the idea of speaking in tongues. There was so much excitement about the members of the community who apparently had this gift that St. Paul found it necessary to remind them not to overlook the diversity of gifts found among them, starting with the gift of faith. Those gifted with interpretation of tongues, or with healing, would attract more attention than those praying quietly at home, but that did not mean that anyone's gifts were more important than those of anyone else. All spiritual gifts are from the same Spirit.

REFLECT

What are your spiritual gifts? How are they different from the ones you have experienced at other times in your life?

Pray for the grace to discern the spiritual gifts that are particular to times of isolation. How have you experienced these gifts?

Pray for an increase in the gifts of wisdom, knowledge, and faith.

How can you grow closer to God in times of isolation? Pray for the grace to recognize the opportunities.

Luke 10:38–42

As they continued their journey he entered a village where a woman whose name was Martha welcomed him. She had a sister named Mary [who] sat beside the Lord at his feet listening to him speak. Martha, burdened with much serving, came to him and said, "Lord, do you not care that my sister has left me by myself to do the serving? Tell her to help me." The Lord said to her in reply, "Martha, Martha, you are anxious and worried about many things. There is need of only one thing. Mary has chosen the better part and it will not be taken from her."

This passage follows shortly after Jesus has sent out seventy-two disciples "two by two" to preach and heal (Luke 10:1–12) and has told the parable of the Good Samaritan (10:25–37), both examples of active ministries. Mary, by contrast, is called to contemplation, even to the point of neglecting family obligations. For a woman to sit at the feet of a rabbi, listening and learning, was unheard of, even scandalous. Mary wasn't isolated in the sense that a sick person may be, but she was certainly singled out by her unconventional response. Her call to contemplation was strong enough to overcome all such obstacles.

A call to contemplation can come at any time in life, even when a person is isolated by pain.

REFLECT

Sit with Mary and listen to Jesus. What is he saying to you?

How does spending more time alone suggest different ways you might pray?

Psalm 42:2–6, 12

As the deer longs for streams of water,
so my soul longs for you, O God.
My soul thirsts for God, the living God.
When can I enter and see the face of God?
My tears have been my bread day and night,
as they ask me every day, "Where is your God?"
Those times I recall
as I pour out my soul,
When I would cross over to the shrine of the
        Mighty One,
to the house of God,
Amid loud cries of thanksgiving,
with the multitude keeping festival.
Why are you downcast, my soul;
why do you groan within me?
Wait for God, for I shall again praise him,
my savior and my God.

An excerpt from this psalm was recited in the "prayers at the foot of the altar" in the pre–Vatican II Mass. In the archaic formal language then in use, the priest proclaimed "I will go in unto the altar of God, unto God who giveth joy to my youth."

Here, the psalmist longs for that same joy of the Temple worship from which he is exiled, and for all the joys he experienced when he was free to worship. Yet deep in his depression, he trusts that God will deliver him and that he will once again join the community in praise.

During the COVID-19 pandemic, many churches were closed for varying periods of time. Even after they reopened with safety precautions, many older adults did not feel safe worshipping in a crowd. Where the sick and homebound had once had few alternatives except perhaps a televised Mass from a distant city at 6 a.m., one good thing that came out of the pandemic was the increasing availability of a livestreamed Mass, from a local parish or a large cathedral, on Sundays and weekdays. Technology, so often maligned, has become an instrument of grace for many.

REFLECT

When have you experienced joy in worship? What made it joyful?

How can technology help make your prayer more fruitful?

When participating in a livestreamed Mass, pray the prayer for spiritual communion; here are two versions:

Prayer of St. Alphonsus Liguori for Spiritual Communion

My Jesus, I believe that You are present in the Most Holy Sacrament. I love You above all things, and I desire to receive You into my soul. Since I cannot at this moment receive you sacramentally, come at least spiritually into my heart. I embrace You as if You were already there, and unite myself wholly to You. Never permit me to be separated from You. Amen.

A Modern Version
Jesus, I love you, and I want to love you more.
I believe you are truly present in the sacrament of the altar,
    and I'm sorry that I can't be there to receive you in
    person.
But I am immensely grateful for the technology that allows
    me to share in this Eucharist, even though I can't
    be there.
And so, unworthy as I am, I ask you to give me the graces
    of spiritual communion.
Let me reach out and take them into my heart and soul;
savor them, live them, and with your help share them with
    others.
And never let me take your gifts for granted.
Thank you, Lord.

9

Sadness and Grief

We often think of grief as the powerful emotion that accompanies death, but in fact we grieve many things: the loss of a job, our lost youth, a broken relationship, and all the things we can no longer do when we are seriously ill, disabled, or bereaved. Sadness can be more like a chronic ache than the stabbing sensation of grief, but it isn't always easy to draw the line between them. The Scripture passages in this chapter reflect different degrees of negative feelings.

Matthew 19:16–22

Now someone approached him and said, "Teacher, what good must I do to gain eternal life?" He answered him, "Why do you ask me about the good? There is only One who is good. If you wish to enter into life, keep the commandments." He asked him, "Which ones?" And Jesus replied, "'You shall not kill; you shall not commit adultery; you shall not steal; you shall not bear false witness; honor your father and your mother'; and 'you shall love your neighbor as yourself.'" The young man said to him, "All of these I have observed. What do I still lack?" Jesus said to him, "If you wish to be perfect, go, sell what you have and give to [the] poor, and you will have treasure in heaven. Then come, follow me." When the young man heard this statement, he went away sad, for he had many possessions.

The NABR notes to this chapter explain that "to be perfect is demanded of all Christians. . . . In the case of this man, it involves selling his possessions and giving to the poor." The implication is that we may be called in different ways; some may rejoice, and others may be saddened by what is asked.

REFLECT

Experience the sadness of this young man. Why is he sad? What advice would you give him?

What is Jesus asking you to give up? Could it be some of the freedom that comes with good health? Is it OK to be sad about that? Why or why not?

Listen to Jesus saying to you, "Come, follow me."

Psalm 22:2–6, 12, 20–26

My God, my God, why have you abandoned me?
Why so far from my call for help,
from my cries of anguish?
My God, I call by day, but you do not answer;
by night, but I have no relief.
Yet you are enthroned as the Holy One;
you are the glory of Israel.
In you our fathers trusted;
they trusted and you rescued them.
To you they cried out and they escaped;
in you they trusted and were not disappointed.
Do not stay far from me,
for trouble is near,
and there is no one to help.
But you, LORD, do not stay far off;
my strength, come quickly to help me.
Deliver my soul from the sword,
my life from the grip of the dog.
Save me from the lion's mouth,
my poor life from the horns of wild bulls.
Then I will proclaim your name to my brethren;
in the assembly I will praise you:
"You who fear the LORD, give praise!
All descendants of Jacob, give honor;
show reverence, all descendants of Israel!
For he has not spurned or disdained
the misery of this poor wretch,

Did not turn away from me,
but heard me when I cried out.
I will offer praise in the great assembly;
my vows I will fulfill before those who fear him."

This very long psalm moves from an anguished lament through memories of God's past mercies to a conclusion of effusive praise: from sadness to hope.

Most Christians are familiar with the Gospel narratives where Jesus prayed the first line of this psalm on the cross (Mark 15:34; Matthew 27:46). His difficulty in breathing would have prevented him from reciting any more, but we may be reasonably certain that, like all observant Jews of his time, he knew all the psalms, including this psalmist's passage from despair to hope.

REFLECT

Pray this psalm aloud. Pause where the psalmist moves from his own despair to the mercy of God. How could this happen?

Imagine yourself at the foot of the cross as Jesus calls out the first line of this psalm. Who else is there? Who else hears it? How do you feel?

When have you felt abandoned? Talk to God about it.

Matthew 27:57–61

When it was evening, there came a rich man from Arimathea named Joseph, who was himself a disciple of Jesus. He went to Pilate and asked for the body of Jesus; then Pilate ordered it to be handed over. Taking the body, Joseph wrapped it [in] clean linen and laid it in his new tomb that he had hewn in the rock. Then he rolled a huge stone across the entrance to the tomb and departed. But Mary Magdalene and the other Mary remained sitting there, facing the tomb.

At the foot of the cross when Jesus died were Mary his mother, Mary Magdalene, and "the disciple whom Jesus loved" (John 19:26). Three people who had been closest to him in life were closest in death. Overwhelmed with grief, they were deprived of even the opportunity to care for his body in accordance with the rituals prescribed by Jewish law, as it was snatched away by Joseph of Arimathea and placed behind a huge stone. Because it was the eve of the Sabbath, there was nothing they could do except try to find their way to their lodgings and mourn in privacy.

REFLECT

Imagine what that Sabbath was like, from sundown on Friday until sundown on Saturday. Where did Mary, John, and Mary Magdalene spend the night and the next day? How did they console one another?

Luke 23:56 says, "They rested on the Sabbath." What do you think that "rest" was like? What did they think about, and talk about, on Saturday?

Find a representation of Michelangelo's *Pietà* on the internet or in an art book. What emotions do you see on the face of Mary? What can you say to console her? Can you ask her to console you?

Feel the weight on Mary's arms as she holds the heavy body of her dead son. Where does she get the strength to do this? Where can you find the strength to bear your own suffering?

10

Trauma

People who have experienced trauma often have difficulty processing their emotions, let alone praying about them. Terrible memories, hurts too deep for words, paralyzing fears, inability to ask for help—these can all seem like insurmountable barriers to connecting with God. The Scripture passages in this chapter express the feelings of some who have been there before us.

Psalm 88:2–19

Lord, the God of my salvation, I call out by day;
at night I cry aloud in your presence.
Let my prayer come before you;
incline your ear to my cry.
For my soul is filled with troubles;
my life draws near to Sheol.
I am reckoned with those who go down to the pit;
I am like a warrior without strength.
My couch is among the dead,

like the slain who lie in the grave.
You remember them no more;
they are cut off from your influence.
You plunge me into the bottom of the pit,
into the darkness of the abyss.
Your wrath lies heavy upon me;
all your waves crash over me.
Because of you my acquaintances shun me;
you make me loathsome to them;
Caged in, I cannot escape;
my eyes grow dim from trouble.
All day I call on you, LORD;
I stretch out my hands to you.
Do you work wonders for the dead?
Do the shades arise and praise you?
Is your mercy proclaimed in the grave,
your faithfulness among those who have perished?
Are your marvels declared in the darkness,
your righteous deeds in the land of oblivion?
But I cry out to you, LORD;
in the morning my prayer comes before you.
Why do you reject my soul, LORD,
and hide your face from me?
I have been mortally afflicted since youth;
I have borne your terrors and I am made numb.
Your wrath has swept over me;
your terrors have destroyed me.
All day they surge round like a flood;
from every side they encircle me.
Because of you friend and neighbor shun me;
my only friend is darkness.

Archaeologists in Jerusalem have excavated a first-century complex that is believed to have been the house of the high priest. Deep, dry cisterns below ground level are believed to have been used to hold prisoners for short periods. There is a local tradition that Jesus was kept in one of these cisterns overnight, and that while there he prayed Psalm 88.

In one of these spaces, there is a tiny altar, surrounded by reproductions of Psalm 88 in many languages. The English translation, from the Jerusalem Bible, is a searing cry of desolation by one "numbered among those who go down into the pit . . . a man alone, down among the dead," who complains to God, "You have turned my friends and neighbors against me, and darkness is my one companion left."

This psalm is unusual in that it does not follow the typical progression from desolation to hope in God. It ends in darkness. Jesus, praying this psalm after having accepted his own suffering (see Luke 22:39–42), now in the darkest hour of the night, takes on the suffering of all prisoners—those confined within concrete walls and those whose prison is their own mind. He shares the pain of those who have no hope, the darkness of those who see no light, the loneliness of those who have been abandoned by all.

REFLECT

Be with Jesus in the dark cistern during the night. Imagine him sharing your pain—whatever it is. Ask him for the grace to surface your deepest feelings and seek help when you need it.

Pray Psalm 22 (in chapter 9) and linger with the progression from despair to hope.

Pray for all those who are unjustly imprisoned, for women and children in abusive relationships, for victims of violence and war.

Psalm 137:1–6

By the rivers of Babylon
there we sat weeping
when we remembered Zion.
On the poplars in its midst
we hung up our harps.
For there our captors asked us
for the words of a song;
Our tormentors, for joy:
"Sing for us a song of Zion!"
But how could we sing a song of the LORD
in a foreign land?

If I forget you, Jerusalem,
may my right hand forget.
May my tongue stick to my palate
if I do not remember you,
If I do not exalt Jerusalem
beyond all my delights.

The psalmist expresses the collective trauma of the people after the destruction of the Temple and the exile of the population of Jerusalem to Babylon, in 587 BC. Recognizing their inability to feign emotions they do not feel, he urges them to happy memories—not the scenes of death and destruction, but Jerusalem as it was in good times.

REFLECT

When have you been urged to "look on the bright side" or words to that effect? Pray for the grace to be honest about your feelings.

How does the Babylonian exile compare with the displaced migrants of our own time? Pray for them.

11

Sharing in the Sufferings of Christ

Some Christians find comfort in seeing their pain as an opportunity to share in the sufferings of Christ. It's important not to overthink this. Perhaps the late Walter Burghardt, SJ, put it best: "I do not theologize about the redemptive significance of Calvary; I link a pierced hand to mine."

Others find it difficult to wrap their heads around the details of the Crucifixion; the kind of torture the ancient Romans relied on for deterrence is almost inconceivable to our modern sensibilities. It might be easier to focus on details that aren't quite so far removed from our experience.

Luke 9:22–26

He said, "The Son of Man must suffer greatly and be rejected by the elders, the chief priests, and the scribes, and be killed and on the third day be raised." Then he said to all, "If anyone wishes to come after me, he must deny himself and take up his cross daily and follow me. For whoever wishes to save his life will lose it, but whoever loses his life for my sake will save it. What profit is there for one to gain the whole world yet lose or forfeit himself? Whoever is ashamed of me and of my words, the Son of Man will be ashamed of when he comes in his glory and in the glory of the Father and of the holy angels."

The New American Bible, in its 1970 edition, says that the disciple must "take up his cross *each day* and follow me," a more emphatic assertion that Christianity is a full-time commitment. It isn't enough to be willing to die for Jesus; we must be prepared to suffer every day. Wow.

But there is a more consoling interpretation of this passage: we are called to take up our cross one day at a time.

Many of us who attended Catholic schools, especially in the years before the Second Vatican Council, remember being told to "offer it up" whenever we experienced discomfort or disappointment. The theology behind the idea of vicarious suffering was not explained to us as schoolchildren—and is still debated by theologians—but we absorbed the *feeling* that suffering has redemptive value. Pope John Paul II wrote extensively on this subject and came back to it repeatedly in celebrations of the World Day of the Sick (which since 1995 has been observed on February 11), encouraging us to connect our own sufferings to the redemptive suffering of Christ: to hold that pierced hand.

REFLECT

What is the daily cross you are called to take up? Do you take it up *today*? Willingly or grudgingly? Can you see it as sharing in the sufferings of Christ? Why or why not?

Pray with Isaiah 53:1–12, a long passage in which the prophet foretells the suffering of Christ and sees his vicarious suffering for the benefit of all.

Luke 22:39–46

Then going out he went, as was his custom, to the Mount of Olives, and the disciples followed him. When he arrived at the place he said to them, "Pray that you may not undergo the test." After withdrawing about a stone's throw from them and kneeling, he prayed, saying, "Father, if you are willing, take this cup away from me; still, not my will but yours be done." [And to strengthen him an angel from heaven appeared to him. He was in such agony and he prayed so fervently that his sweat became like drops of blood falling on the ground.] When he rose from prayer and returned to his disciples, he found them sleeping from grief. He said to them, "Why are you sleeping? Get up and pray that you may not undergo the test."

The story of Jesus's agony in the Garden of Gethsemane can be a fruitful meditation on sharing the sufferings of Christ. Clearly, it is more accessible than many parts of the Passion narrative: most of us have known fear, even dread, of something in our immediate future, even to the point of physical suffering. Luke's Gospel is the only one that includes reference to an angel who came "to strengthen him." If we pray to join our sufferings with those of Jesus, we can also expect to be given the strength—the grace—to bear them.

REFLECT

Place yourself in the Garden of Gethsemane. It's a few hours after sunset, and the warmth of a spring day still lingers. You can hear nocturnal insects beginning to call. There are few other sounds, and no people in view, except Jesus, whom you can just make out, a stone's throw away. Are you sleepy after the Passover meal? Can you stay awake for an hour and keep watch with Jesus? Why or why not?

In this place of stillness, imagine that you expect to be arrested in the morning and taken to jail. How do you feel, mentally and physically? What do you want to say to God about it?

Have you been let down or abandoned by someone you counted on to stay with you in your suffering? How did you feel? Can you forgive that person? Why or why not?

John 19:23–25

When the soldiers had crucified Jesus, they took his clothes and divided them into four shares, a share for each soldier. They also took his tunic, but the tunic was seamless, woven in one piece from the top down. So they said to one another, "Let's not tear it, but cast lots for it to see whose it will be," in order that the passage of scripture might be fulfilled: "They divided my garments among them, and for my vesture they cast lots." This is what the soldiers did.

Death by crucifixion was intended to bring shame at least as much as to deter. Jesus is usually depicted wearing only a loincloth, although that was a concession denied to ordinary criminals, who were usually raised up naked in the midst of a howling crowd.

REFLECT

If you have ever experienced a colonoscopy, you may have had to walk from the dressing room wearing nothing but a short paper gown, open in the back, toward a trio of doctor, nurse, and technician, ready to anesthetize you and insert a camera into your most intimate parts. Did you feel uncomfortable? Humiliated? Powerless? How do you imagine Jesus felt when he was stripped of his clothing?

Matthew 27:45–50

From noon onward darkness came over the whole land until three in the afternoon. And about three o'clock Jesus cried out in a loud voice, "*Eli, Eli, lema sabachthani?*" which means, "My God, my God, why have you forsaken me?" Some of the bystanders who heard it said, "This one is calling for Elijah." Immediately one of them ran to get a sponge; he soaked it in wine, and putting it on a reed, gave it to him to drink. But the rest said, "Wait, let us see if Elijah comes to save him." But Jesus cried out again in a loud voice, and gave up his spirit.

The Evangelist quotes the Hebrew version of a well-known line from Psalm 22. Although Aramaic was the language of the common people, educated Jews would have been familiar with the Hebrew texts, read in the synagogues, as well as studied and discussed. Not all the "bystanders," however, understood the allusion, which is not surprising, given that Jews who came up to Jerusalem for the Passover spoke many languages. Apart from mistaking "Eli" for "Elijah," they would not have recognized the first line of a psalm that begins in desperation and ends with confidence in God's goodness. Even in his last agony, Jesus was misunderstood.

REFLECT

When have you been misunderstood when speaking about your pain? Pray for the grace to forgive the misunderstanding.

When has God heard you when you cried out?

Review the longer excerpt from Psalm 22 in chapter 9. How do these verses speak to you now?

1 Peter 4:12–13

Beloved, do not be surprised that a trial by fire is occurring among you, as if something strange were happening to you. But rejoice to the extent that you share in the sufferings of Christ, so that when his glory is revealed you may also rejoice exultantly.

This passage is generally understood as referring to persecution. It isn't difficult to apply this thinking by analogy to "trials" other than persecution: the suffering that comes from physical pain or mental anguish. Jesus suffered both, and then rose in glory. So, as we "share in the sufferings of Christ," our reward will be great.

REFLECT

What does it mean to "rejoice" in sharing in the sufferings of Christ? Is Peter exaggerating for dramatic effect, or is there a paradox here that goes to the heart of the Passion and Resurrection of Jesus?

12

Stillness

There is a difference between silence and stillness. Silence is the absence of sound around us, which is increasingly difficult to find. We are so inured to environmental noise (traffic, sirens, raised voices, loud car radios) that some people walk around listening to playlists through headphones, filling the silence with different kinds of sound. Noise is the default. Finding a silent atmosphere for prayer can be a distinct challenge.

Stillness is another matter altogether. Whatever is going on around us, even if we are fortunate enough to be in a quiet park or an empty church, we all have internal background noise: our thoughts about what just happened or what may happen today or tomorrow; imaginary conversations about an imminent event or the continuation of a quarrel; our fears and anxieties. Quieting this internal noise can be helped by silence—anyone who has made a silent retreat can relate to that—but doing so is not dependent on silence. Tuning out unnecessary noise (such as taking off the headphones) is a good start, but the essential mindset is the desire to listen to God.

Listening may be difficult when pain seems to drown out everything else. The Scriptures in this chapter suggest the connection between an attitude of stillness and the ability to hear God's call, especially in times of suffering. There are no magic words to achieve interior stillness, but we start with the desire to listen.

1 Kings 19:11–13

Then the LORD said: Go out and stand on the mountain before the LORD; the LORD will pass by. There was a strong and violent wind rending the mountains and crushing rocks before the LORD—but the LORD was not in the wind; after the wind, an earthquake—but the LORD was not in the earthquake; after the earthquake, fire—but the LORD was not in the fire; after the fire, a light silent sound.

The 1970 edition of the New American Bible has a more poetic translation of that last verse: "After the fire there was a tiny whispering sound." The New Revised Standard Version refers to "a still small voice." Both of these alternatives seem to me to convey more clearly that Elijah heard the voice of God in the stillness.

Elijah's encounter with God occurred at a tumultuous time, recounted in 1 Kings 13:22–19:8. He had humiliated, defeated, and killed the false prophets of Baal and then prayed for rain that ended a lengthy drought. The evil queen Jezebel, enraged by these events, swore to kill Elijah, who was forced to flee for his life. Discouraged by what he perceived as the failure of his prophetic mission, he begged God for death. Instead, God sent him to "the mountain of God, Horeb" (Sinai) where he was given a new understanding of how God speaks. Although wind and storms and other natural phenomena may suggest the power of God, only the "tiny whispering sound" conveys the mystery.

REFLECT

When have you felt surrounded by dark clouds? Can you listen for the voice of the Lord in the darkness?

What are you fleeing from? Can you pause to listen?

Are you afraid of listening to God's voice? Why or why not?

The name *Elijah* means "the Lord is my God." What does that phrase mean to you?

Pray with Matthew 1:18–24, in which Joseph heard the
Lord's call in a dream and "did as the angel of the Lord had
commanded him." How does stillness help us understand
what God is calling us to, here and now?

———————

Psalm 46:2–12

God is our refuge and our strength,
an ever-present help in distress.
Thus we do not fear, though earth be shaken
and mountains quake to the depths of the sea,
Though its waters rage and foam
and mountains totter at its surging.
Streams of the river gladden the city of God,
the holy dwelling of the Most High.
God is in its midst; it shall not be shaken;
God will help it at break of day.
Though nations rage and kingdoms totter,
he utters his voice and the earth melts.
The LORD of hosts is with us;
our stronghold is the God of Jacob.
Come and see the works of the LORD,
who has done fearsome deeds on earth;
Who stops wars to the ends of the earth,
breaks the bow, splinters the spear,

and burns the shields with fire;
"Be still and know that I am God!
I am exalted among the nations,
exalted on the earth."
The LORD of hosts is with us;
our stronghold is the God of Jacob.

The psalmist vividly describes all kinds of tumult: "mountains quake to the depths of the sea"; "nations rage and kingdoms totter"; natural disasters and human wars. Then, suddenly, a vivid contrast: "Be still and know that I am God!"

REFLECT

What are the "quaking mountains" or "raging streams" in your life? Where do you hear God's voice?

Pray with Psalm 131. Pray for the grace to still your soul.

Paraphrase of Psalm 23 by an anonymous Japanese Christian

The Lord is my pace-setter;
I shall not rush
He makes me stop and rest
For quiet intervals;
He provides me with images of stillness

Which restore my serenity
He leads me in ways of efficiency
Through calmness of mind
And his guidance is peace.
Even though I have many things
To accomplish each day
I will not fret, for his presence is here
His timelessness, His all-importance
Will keep me in balance
He prepares refreshment and renewal
In the midst of my activity
By anointing my head with
His oil of tranquility.
My cup of joyous energy overflows.
Surely harmony and effectiveness
Shall be the fruit of my hours
For I shall walk in the pace of my Lord
And dwell in his house forever.

REFLECT

What are your "images of stillness"? Sit with them. Talk to God about them.

Sometimes it's our minds, even more than our bodies, that need to "stop and rest for quiet intervals." How can you make that part of your routine?

What is the "pace of the Lord" at this time in your life?

13

Trust

Mark 10:46–52

They came to Jericho. And as he was leaving Jericho with his disciples and a sizable crowd, Bartimaeus, a blind man, the son of Timaeus, sat by the roadside begging. On hearing that it was Jesus of Nazareth, he began to cry out and say, "Jesus, son of David, have pity on me." And many rebuked him, telling him to be silent. But he kept calling out all the more, "Son of David, have pity on me." Jesus stopped and said, "Call him." So they called the blind man, saying to him, "Take courage; get up, he is calling you." He threw aside his cloak, sprang up, and came to Jesus. Jesus said to him in reply, "What do you want me to do for you?" The blind man replied to him, "Master, I want to see." Jesus told him, "Go your way; your faith has saved you." Immediately he received his sight and followed him on the way.

It isn't always easy to be honest in our prayer. Christians understand that suffering is part of the human condition and that Jesus clearly told us so: "Take up [your] cross daily and follow me" (Luke 9:23). But accepting that reality sometimes leads us to a kind of fatalism: if God has sent this suffering, I must accept it; I can't ask for healing.

Bartimaeus had no such hesitation. He asked for healing and Jesus said, "Your faith has saved you." We can't necessarily expect a miraculous cure, but that isn't the only way God heals.

REFLECT

Imagine you are Bartimaeus. What does it feel like to be blind? To beg? To be told to shut up when you ask for help? How are you able to persist?

What do you want God to do for you?

Pray for the grace to be honest with God.

Psalm 86:1–7

A prayer of David.
Incline your ear, LORD, and answer me,
for I am poor and oppressed.
Preserve my life, for I am devoted;
save your servant who trusts in you.
You are my God;
be gracious to me, Lord;
to you I call all the day.
Gladden the soul of your servant;
to you, Lord, I lift up my soul.
Lord, you are good and forgiving,
most merciful to all who call on you.
LORD, hear my prayer;
listen to my cry for help.
On the day of my distress I call to you,
for you will answer me.

REFLECT

After repeated pleas for help, the psalmist concludes with
the confident assertion: "you will answer me." How did he
move from feeling "poor and oppressed" to trust? Can you
make the same leap of faith? Why or why not?

When has God been "gracious" to you? When has God "gladdened" your soul? What other words or phrases in this psalm speak to you?

Psalm 23

Psalm 23 is so familiar that many people find it hard to get to the meaning or to see its application to their own situation. In addition, because this psalm is so often used at funerals, it is easy to overlook its emphasis on life. The NABR and the New Revised Standard Version (NRSV), the two modern translations most commonly used in the United States, are alike in emphasizing that God's goodness is present "all the days of my life." Trusting in the Lord in times of trouble is not a matter of words but of a state of mind:

NABR
The LORD is my shepherd;
there is nothing I lack.
In green pastures he makes me lie down;
to still waters he leads me;
he restores my soul.
He guides me along right paths
for the sake of his name.

Even though I walk through the valley of the shadow
     of death,
I will fear no evil, for you are with me;
your rod and your staff comfort me.
You set a table before me
in front of my enemies;
You anoint my head with oil;
my cup overflows.
Indeed, goodness and mercy will pursue me
all the days of my life;
I will dwell in the house of the LORD
for endless days.

NRSV
The LORD is my shepherd, I shall not want.
He makes me lie down in green pastures;
he leads me beside still waters;
he restores my soul.
He leads me in right paths
for his name's sake.
Even though I walk through the darkest valley,
I fear no evil;
for you are with me;
your rod and your staff—
they comfort me.
You prepare a table before me
in the presence of my enemies;
you anoint my head with oil;
my cup overflows.
Surely goodness and mercy shall follow me

all the days of my life,
and I shall dwell in the house of the LORD
my whole life long.

REFLECT

Pray with each of these versions separately, at different times, focusing on the language. Which one speaks to you? How?

This psalm has been set to music in many different settings. Some may be found in parish hymnals, others on YouTube or other digital formats. Find one and listen.

Luke 1:39–45

During those days Mary set out and traveled to the hill country in haste to a town of Judah, where she entered the house of Zechariah and greeted Elizabeth. When Elizabeth heard Mary's greeting, the infant leaped in her womb, and Elizabeth, filled with the holy Spirit, cried out in a loud voice and said, "Most blessed are you among women, and blessed is the fruit of your womb. And how does this happen to me, that the mother of my Lord should come to me? For at the moment the sound of your greeting reached my ears, the infant in my womb leaped for joy. Blessed are you who believed that what was spoken to you by the Lord would be fulfilled."

It can be difficult to identify with some of the most familiar personalities in Scripture, to get inside their heads, so to speak, as we are encouraged to do in the Ignatian tradition of praying with Scripture. Mary may be the most difficult of all, since Catholics in particular have been taught from childhood to see her as the embodiment of all virtue, a person unique in perfection. It takes an effort to imagine her as a real human being, a pregnant teenager, trusting in God in a difficult, even scandalous, situation. Yet Elizabeth, greeting her with joy, presents her in simple human terms, as one "who believed that what was spoken to you by the Lord would be fulfilled."

REFLECT

Eavesdrop on Mary and Elizabeth as they prepare for the birth of their children, six months apart. How do they show their trust in God? How can you show your trust in God?

Pray with Psalm 28:6–9, in which the psalmist, probably King David, moves from lament to praising "the Lord . . . in whom my heart trusts."

14

Gratitude

Gratitude is not the first thing that comes to mind when we're sick or grieving. It's much easier to focus our prayer on what we *want* than on what we have received. Worse, there can be a strong temptation to blame God for giving us pain instead of relief, sorrow instead of joy. "Why me?"

Yet gratitude is an essential element of a mature spirituality. St. Ignatius of Loyola thought that ingratitude was the worst sin because it underlay all others. He saw pride, anger, lust, and all the other capital sins as originating in a lack of gratitude to God for all that he has given us. The Ignatian Examen (chapter 17) begins with gratitude and directs our attention to all the things in our daily lives we can be thankful for.

Ignatius was not alone in this teaching. St. Francis of Assisi drafted a rule in 1221 for his brothers that began "We thank you for yourself," addressing "the Lord God who has given and gives to each of us our whole body, our whole soul and our whole life."

When it's hard to feel grateful, this can be a good place to start: the existence of a loving God and our own existence. This may lead to gratitude for the gift of faith and the urge to pray—and from that to simpler, everyday blessings. No matter how bad we feel, it's possible to thank God for beautiful weather, for a comforting letter or phone call, for the skill and dedication of a doctor or professional caregiver, for the sacrifice of a family member, for today's Gospel, for a comfortable pillow, a warm blanket, the daily newspaper. Pain should not obscure our gratitude for our more permanent gifts such as the good people in our lives, our intelligence, our skills, our education, and the doors these gifts have opened for us. The possibilities are as varied as every individual.

Focusing on small daily blessings as well as lasting ones can lead us to a deeper gratitude as we learn to find grace in all things, even the most serious trials.

Psalm 16:1–2, 5–11

Keep me safe, O God;
in you I take refuge.
I say to the LORD,
you are my Lord,
you are my only good.
LORD, my allotted portion and my cup,
you have made my destiny secure.
Pleasant places were measured out for me;
fair to me indeed is my inheritance.
I bless the LORD who counsels me;
even at night my heart exhorts me.
I keep the LORD always before me;
with him at my right hand, I shall never be shaken.
Therefore my heart is glad, my soul rejoices;
my body also dwells secure,
For you will not abandon my soul to Sheol
nor let your devout one see the pit.
You will show me the path to life,
abounding joy in your presence,
the delights at your right hand forever.

Inheritance in ancient Israel referred to land, the foundation of the agrarian economy and the determinant of a family's place in society. In our time, we can read verse 6 metaphorically, thanking God for our own circumstances,

remembering that all is gift. In times of pain or loss, it may
be difficult to recite that verse; if so, recall the psalmist's trust
that God "will not abandon my soul."

REFLECT

What are you most grateful for today?

What are the more permanent gifts you can thank God for?

Can you see the Lord as your "allotted portion and . . . cup"?
Why or why not?

If you are awake at night, to what does your heart
exhort you?

In the next two psalms, the psalmist thanks God for rescuing
him not only from severe distress or mortal danger but also
from near despair. Sometimes healing the spirit is at least as
important as relief from physical pain.

Psalm 34:2–10, 19–20

I will bless the LORD at all times;
his praise shall be always in my mouth.
My soul will glory in the LORD;

Let the poor hear and be glad.
Magnify the LORD with me;
and let us exalt his name together.
I sought the LORD, and he answered me,
delivered me from all my fears.
Look to him and be radiant,
and your faces may not blush for shame.
This poor one cried out and the LORD heard,
and from all his distress he saved him.
The angel of the LORD encamps
around those who fear him, and he saves them.
Taste and see that the LORD is good;
blessed is the stalwart one who takes refuge in him.
Fear the LORD, you his holy ones;
nothing is lacking to those who fear him.
The LORD is close to the brokenhearted,
saves those whose spirit is crushed.
Many are the troubles of the righteous,
but the LORD delivers him from them all.

Psalm 116

I love the LORD, who listened
to my voice in supplication,
Who turned an ear to me
on the day I called.
I was caught by the cords of death;
the snares of Sheol had seized me;

I felt agony and dread.
Then I called on the name of the LORD,
"O LORD, save my life!"

Gracious is the LORD and righteous;
yes, our God is merciful.
The LORD protects the simple;
I was helpless, but he saved me.
Return, my soul, to your rest;
the LORD has been very good to you.
For my soul has been freed from death,
my eyes from tears, my feet from stumbling.
I shall walk before the LORD
in the land of the living.

I kept faith, even when I said,
"I am greatly afflicted!"
I said in my alarm,
"All men are liars!"
How can I repay the LORD
for all the great good done for me?
I will raise the cup of salvation
and call on the name of the LORD.
I will pay my vows to the LORD
in the presence of all his people.
Dear in the eyes of the LORD
is the death of his devoted.
LORD, I am your servant,
your servant, the child of your maidservant;
you have loosed my bonds.
I will offer a sacrifice of praise

and call on the name of the LORD.
I will pay my vows to the LORD
in the presence of all his people,
In the courts of the house of the LORD,
in your midst, O Jerusalem.
Hallelujah!

REFLECT

When have you "sought the Lord"? Do you believe he will "deliver [you] from all [your] fears"? Why or why not?

When have you felt "greatly afflicted"? What did you say to God about it? How can you call on the name of the Lord now?

Most of us may not be able to place ourselves in the shoes of the ancient worshipper in the Temple shouting "Hallelujah." How can you praise God, here and now?

15

Compassion

When we are sick or grieving, it's easy for our suffering to become the center of our universe, crowding out all other thoughts and feelings. It's hard, in these circumstances, to think about the needs of others. Paradoxically, if we succeed in turning our attention to the pain of other people, we can better deal with our own pain.

Luke 23:33, 39–43

When they came to the place called the Skull, they crucified him and the criminals there, one on his right, the other on his left. . . . Now one of the criminals hanging there reviled Jesus, saying, "Are you not the Messiah? Save yourself and us." The other, however, rebuking him, said in reply, "Have you no fear of God, for you are subject to the same condemnation? And indeed, we have been condemned justly, for the sentence we received corresponds

to our crimes, but this man has done nothing criminal."
Then he said, "Jesus, remember me when you come into
your kingdom." He replied to him, "Amen, I say to you,
today you will be with me in Paradise."

Jesus is our model in all things. Moments before dying (Luke
23:44), he used his last breaths to console one who needed it
desperately.

REFLECT

Ask Jesus to remember you. Listen to his response.

Do you find it hard to empathize with the suffering of others
when you are in pain? If so, why? How can you show
compassion to others in pain?

2 Corinthians 1:3–7

Blessed be the God and Father of our Lord Jesus Christ,
the Father of compassion and God of all encouragement,
who encourages us in our every affliction, so that we may
be able to encourage those who are in any affliction with
the encouragement with which we ourselves are encouraged by God. For as Christ's sufferings overflow to us, so

through Christ does our encouragement also overflow. If we are afflicted, it is for your encouragement and salvation; if we are encouraged, it is for your encouragement, which enables you to endure the same sufferings that we suffer. Our hope for you is firm, for we know that as you share in the sufferings, you also share in the encouragement.

Paul's "afflictions" were constant: beatings, stonings, shipwrecks, hunger and thirst, insults, and many "brushes with death," to say nothing of the "angel of Satan" that tormented him (2 Corinthians 11:23; 12:7). He experienced all these trials in union with Christ, and thus as consolations (an alternative translation of the Greek word here rendered "encouragement") and as a call to console others.

As Paul understood, our own afflictions can help us better understand how others are suffering, and in so doing step outside ourselves.

REFLECT

Who in your life needs encouragement or consolation? What are some of the ways you can meet these needs?

Focus on someone you interact with on a regular basis: a family member, a friend, or a caregiver. Hold that person in your mind. Pray for the grace to discern what they are suffering, what they need. The next time you see that person, greet them with a smile and a sincere question about their well-being. Don't just ask "How are you?" That's a greeting, not a question. Present that person to God in your prayer and ask that he or she be blessed.

Tomorrow, think of a different person and repeat the exercise.

Pray with 1 Kings 17:8–16, where the widow of Zarephath, dying of starvation, finds the strength to aid the prophet Elijah.

---

1 Corinthians 13:1–13

If I speak in human and angelic tongues but do not have love, I am a resounding gong or a clashing cymbal. And if I have the gift of prophecy and comprehend all mysteries and all knowledge; if I have all faith so as to move mountains but do not have love, I am nothing. If I give away everything I own, and if I hand my body over so that I may boast but do not have love, I gain nothing. Love is patient, love is kind. It is not jealous, [love] is not pompous, it is not inflated, it is not rude, it does not seek its own interests, it is not quick-tempered, it does not brood over injury, it does not rejoice over wrongdoing but rejoices with the truth. It bears all things, believes all things, hopes all things, endures all things. Love never fails. If there are prophecies, they will be brought to nothing; if tongues, they will cease; if knowledge, it will be brought to nothing. For we know partially and we prophesy partially, but when the perfect comes, the partial will pass away. When I was a child, I used to talk as a child, think as a child, reason as a child; when I became a man, I put aside childish things. At present we see indistinctly, as in a mirror, but then face to face. At present I know partially; then I shall know fully, as I am fully known. So faith, hope, love remain, these three; but the greatest of these is love.

My ninth-grade religion teacher required our class to memorize this passage and recite it. The pre–Vatican II translation used the word *charity* instead of *love*, which greatly diminished the message to a group of fourteen-year-olds who were constantly being admonished to give generously "to the missions" and other worthy causes. Our twenty-first-century understanding of Christian love is much broader and deeper; without it, Christianity makes no sense.

REFLECT

Review the adjectives describing what love is and is not. Which ones resonate with you? Which do not?

Ask St. Paul how he would describe love to a person who is in pain.

Pray for the grace to open your heart to the love of Christ.

16

Hope of Eternal Life

The early Christians thought of death as "falling asleep"; eternal life was as real to them as what they planned to do the following week. Our culture, in contrast, is largely in denial about death, and we focus on amassing material things and enjoying the pleasures of the present moment. Death is the end. This worldview has little to offer someone in pain.

A person who has lost someone they love may find comfort in the belief in eternal life—a belief founded on the Gospels, not on some of the saccharine clichés with which well-meaning friends often respond to a death. A person who is seriously ill, consciously or unconsciously influenced by the prevailing culture, may want to think about anything other than death. Yet death is part of life, and for the believer the portal to another life, unmarred by sin, suffering, or mutability.

John 14:1–4

"Do not let your hearts be troubled. You have faith in God; have faith also in me. In my Father's house there are many dwelling places. If there were not, would I have told you that I am going to prepare a place for you? And if I go and prepare a place for you, I will come back again and take you to myself, so that where I am you also may be. Where [I] am going you know the way."

In all four Gospels, Jesus repeatedly promised eternal life to those who believe in him. This passage is part of the Last Discourse, which John places on the night before Jesus died. While the last sentence reminds the disciples that they will have to share in the sufferings of Jesus to share in his Resurrection, it leaves no doubt that this is "so that where I am you also may be."

REFLECT

How do you "know the way" to eternal life? What does it mean in the context of your present situation?

Pray with Luke 2:22–32, in which Simeon greets the infant Jesus with a prayer reflecting his peaceful readiness for eternal life.

Pray with Luke 18:28–30, one promise of eternal life. What have you given up to follow Jesus?

———————————

John 12:24–26

Amen, amen, I say to you, unless a grain of wheat falls to the ground and dies, it remains just a grain of wheat; but if it dies, it produces much fruit. Whoever loves his life loses it, and whoever hates his life in this world will preserve it for eternal life. Whoever serves me must follow me, and where I am, there also will my servant be.

The Gospel of Luke has a somewhat milder statement corresponding to verse 25: "Whoever seeks to preserve his life will lose it, but whoever loses it will save it" (Luke 17:33; see also Matthew 10:39 and Mark 8:35). John's use of the word *hates* is striking, as it emphasizes the contrast between our temporary life in this world and the eternal life promised to those who believe. The metaphor of the grain of wheat would have been understood more readily in an agrarian society, but even for us the meaning is clear: the death of our mortal life leads to immortality.

REFLECT

How do you understand the last sentence of this passage?

What are you trying to "preserve" in this life? Pray for the grace to let go.

Wisdom 3:1–9

The souls of the righteous are in the hand of God,
and no torment shall touch them.
They seemed, in the view of the foolish, to be dead;
and their passing away was thought an affliction
and their going forth from us, utter destruction.
But they are in peace.
For if to others, indeed, they seem punished,
yet is their hope full of immortality;
Chastised a little, they shall be greatly blessed,
because God tried them
and found them worthy of himself.
As gold in the furnace, he proved them,
and as sacrificial offerings he took them to himself.
In the time of their judgment they shall shine
and dart about as sparks through stubble;
They shall judge nations and rule over peoples,
and the Lord shall be their King forever.

Those who trust in him shall understand truth,
and the faithful shall abide with him in love:
Because grace and mercy are with his holy ones,
and his care is with the elect.

The book of Wisdom is one of the seven deuterocanonical books (also known as the Apocrypha) that are accepted as part of the Bible by Roman Catholics and Eastern Orthodox Christians, but not by Protestants. The unknown author of Wisdom is believed to have written around the middle of the first century BC, at a time when there was a division of opinion in Israel about life after death. The Sadducees denied the possibility, whereas the legalistic Pharisees considered it the reward of those who obeyed the letter of the law. Here, the author begins with an unequivocal statement that immortality is the reward of "the righteous" and then uses the beautiful images of fire-tried gold and shining, darting sparks to suggest the quality of eternal life.

REFLECT

What does this passage have to say to modern "Sadducees" who believe death is "affliction" or "destruction"?

What does this passage have to say to modern "Pharisees" who define righteousness narrowly?

What does it say to you?

Which of the many images—"gold in the furnace," "sacrificial offerings," "sparks," judges, rulers, people who understand truth—resonates with you? Why?

———————

Luke 20:27–38

Some Sadducees, those who deny that there is a resurrection, came forward and put this question to him, saying, "Teacher, Moses wrote for us, 'If someone's brother dies leaving a wife but no child, his brother must take the wife and raise up descendants for his brother.' Now there were seven brothers; the first married a woman but died childless. Then the second and the third married her, and likewise all the seven died childless. Finally the woman also died. Now at the resurrection whose wife will that woman be? For all seven had been married to her." Jesus said to them, "The children of this age marry and are given in marriage; but those who are deemed worthy to attain to the coming age and to the resurrection of the dead neither marry nor are given in marriage. They can no longer die, for they are like angels; and they are the children of God because they are the ones who will rise. That the dead will rise even Moses made known in the passage about the bush, when he called 'Lord' the God of Abraham, the God of Isaac, and the God of Jacob; and he is not God of the dead, but of the living, for to him all are alive."

The unlucky woman in this story is hypothetical. Lawyers love hypothetical questions. The Socratic method used in most American law schools is founded on them, and advocates revel in using them to portray the worst-case scenarios of their adversaries' positions.

In Jewish tradition, if a man died without children, his brother was required to marry his widow. (She had nothing to say about it.) The Sadducees presented this hypothetical case, based on the law, thinking that Jesus could give no possible answer that could prove the existence of eternal life. Jesus' answer is that they were asking the wrong question.

Eternal life is not a mere continuation of life as we know it, with arguments, legalisms, and questions of status. Eternal life is so glorious, so far beyond our imagining, that it can't be described in ordinary language. The dead are "like angels." What does that mean?

Artists have painted their own images, and philosophers and theologians have speculated on this for millennia. Many people look forward to being reunited with people they love. Some think about pure spirits united with God in a mystical way that we can't imagine; still others think we'll return to the natural state before original sin. The author of the passage from Ecclesiastes in this chapter used various metaphors to describe the dead, but it is clear that they are only metaphors. The fact is, we have no idea what eternal life will be like.

What we do know is that Jesus promised it, over and over. Despite the lack of detail, Jesus's description in this passage is suffused with hope. Eternal life awaits "all who are deemed worthy"—all of us who love him!

REFLECT

How do you imagine eternal life?

Pray with John 3:16, one of the most famous verses in the New Testament. How do you understand the connection between God's love and eternal life?

17

Praying through the Day: The Examen

The Latin word *examen* is usually translated "examination." Spiritual writers in the Ignatian tradition prefer to use the Latin, because for Catholics the word *examination* suggests "examination of conscience": a review to know our sins, especially before confession. The Examen as Ignatius taught it is much more than that: a review of our day to see where God has been active in our lives and how we have responded. This certainly includes acknowledging where we have fallen short in answering God's call, but it also includes recognition of God's presence and our feelings. The Examen helps us develop discernment, gratitude, and hope for the future.

There are many variations on the Examen prayer, but all have five elements in common. The following is a suggested version that might be prayed during a time of pain. It usually takes ten to fifteen minutes, but it can be longer or shorter, depending on the circumstances. It can be prayed at any time of day, looking back over the previous twenty-four hours.

1. **Presence.** Christians are taught that God is always present, no matter where we are or what we're doing. When we're not in church or actively praying, God is a kind of backdrop to daily life whose presence we don't always notice.

   Yet a review of the past day often reveals where God was while we were going about our daily routine, walking or talking on the phone or sitting in a doctor's waiting room. Reviewing the day also brings back the feelings that we experienced, such as anxiety, anger, gratitude, and hope. For this review to bear fruit, we need to be fully present, asking God for the grace to repel distractions and concentrate on the prayer.

   Everyone's life is different, so you can formulate your own questions to pray the Examen. Here are a few that may facilitate this important first step in the prayer:

   • Lord, where were you present in my life this day?

   • Were you in [identify people you interacted with]?

   • Were you in the pain?

   • Were you in the [identify the most powerful emotion of the day, such as sadness, gratitude, or something else]?

- Was I paying attention? If not, what distracted me?

Notice that if your thoughts focused on an important decision you need to make, or on a diagnosis you just received, or on a troubled family member, these are not "distractions" but matters for prayer. In contrast, replaying an unpleasant conversation or thinking about today's (or tomorrow's) to-do list takes the mind away from prayer. "If only" and "what if" are signals to change a line of thought. Pray for the light to identify distractions and let go of them.

2. **The light of the Spirit**. In surfacing our feelings and exploring how we dealt with them, it's important to discern what prompts them. In general, the promptings of the Holy Spirit lead us closer to God and to other people, and they inspire feelings of tranquility and hope. Whatever provokes us to negative feelings, drawing us away from God and other people, is not from the Holy Spirit but from some other source. This is sometimes called the Evil Spirit, but the name doesn't matter; in general, it refers to whatever is the opposite of the Holy Spirit. At this step of the prayer, ask God to send the Holy Spirit to guide you and to give you the grace to distinguish between the Spirit's promptings and the temptations that draw you away from God.

3. **Gratitude.** There are two elements of this step. First, we review our day to identify the gifts of that particular day—maybe it is a favorite food, a long-awaited appointment with a specialist, or something as brief and barely noticeable as a bird singing outside our window or as life changing as a negative test for a deadly disease. Next, we focus on our more permanent gifts, whatever they are: the talents we were born with, the skills we developed, the "lucky breaks" we experienced that weren't luck at all, the people who have enriched our lives; the gift of faith and the ability to pray.

   Every day is different. Every person is different. The one thing that is common to all of us, all the time, is that each new day is a gift. Thank God for it and pray for the grace to unwrap the gift gratefully, mindfully, in a spirit of discovery.

4. **Opportunity for improvement.** Some spiritual writers call this step "Repentance" or "Sorrow for Sin." These terms are too limiting, though. Sin, serious or less so, is essentially a rejection of God's grace. Most of us, if we're honest, realize that we often fail to respond to God's call, not in a sinful way, but just in a way that falls short of a loving response. These experiences don't immediately come to mind the way a serious sin would.

A close inspection of the events and feelings of the day will reveal them. For example:

- Did I complain when I had to wait a little longer than usual? I can pray for the grace of patience.
- Did I rebuff someone trying to help me? I can pray for the grace of gratitude.
- Have I been too quick to criticize? I can pray for the grace to be less judgmental.

5. **Look to the future with hope.** This may be the most difficult step for a person who is seriously ill or grieving the loss of someone they love. It helps to take it one day at a time: What do I hope for *today*? Not a miraculous healing but something simpler, like the consolation that can come with prayer. Some of the things we were grateful for yesterday may suggest hope for today. The hope of eternal life, which as Christians we are promised, may be too vague to provide consolation in the moment. But all the small blessings of daily life are subtle hints of what is promised. Anticipate them with trust and pray for the grace to hope.

It is customary to end the Examen by reciting the Lord's Prayer. If you keep a spiritual journal, enter a few lines about what stood out in today's prayer. Because the spiritual life does not proceed in a straight line but has detours and turns, it's helpful to review the journal entries periodically so you can see the patterns and savor the graces.

18

Praying through Difficult Decisions: Discernment

Illness, loss, and the diminishment that comes with aging often present us with difficult decisions, such as where to live, what treatments may be appropriate, where to seek advice and whether to follow it. In a God-centered life, it's helpful to begin deciding between alternatives by asking: Which alternative leads me closer to God (and other people) and which leads me away? Ignatian spirituality offers useful tools for discerning some answers.

Prayerful decision making has two essential components: careful, thoughtful reasoning, and trust in God. In the Ignatian tradition, there are five suggested steps in discerning both what is reasonable and what God is calling us to do.

1. **Define the question.** This isn't always obvious.
   Consider a person with limited mobility (at any age) who has been advised to move to assisted living. Is the

question "Shall I move to assisted living?" or is it "What is the best way to accommodate my limited mobility so that I can live safely with a good quality of life?" Assisted living might be one answer to the second question, but there may be others, such as making modifications to one's existing house or apartment; hiring home health aides and other helpers; moving in with, or nearer to, a close family member. Every situation is different. It's important not to rush through this step. There may be more than one question, and it might be helpful to follow the succeeding steps for each of them.

2. **Pray for the grace to choose freely.** Specifically, ask for the grace to be neutral, not to be prejudiced in favor of one alternative or the other. St. Ignatius advised thinking of oneself as "a balance at equilibrium, without leaning to either side" (*Spiritual Exercises* 179). A twenty-first-century person might pray for the grace to see the situation as a completely objective, reasonable person might see it. This can be the hardest part of the process, because any major decision is entangled in hopes, fears, and conflicting emotions. A person who has lived for many years in a big house, full of memories as well as rife with hazards, may find the

thought of moving unbearable, yet fear the dangers of living alone.

3. **Pray for the light of the spirit.** Ask God to enlighten and move you toward what he is calling you to do, at this time and place.

4. **Weigh the pros and cons and make a reasoned choice.** To do this step, it's important to have all the facts. You might need to do detailed research before you know what the pros and cons are or, more important, how to weigh them.

This isn't simply a matter of counting up the advantages and disadvantages and going with the higher number. There could be several rational arguments on one side, but one overwhelming consideration on the other. Abraham Lincoln, after all the members of his cabinet had voted "nay," famously ruled, "The ayes have it." Take the time to identify all the advantages and disadvantages of each proposed course of action, note which ones may be unhelpful (such as irrational fears), and do all the necessary research. If you can't find the answers to some of your questions, you may need to list that uncertainty itself among the cons.

Here is an annotated list of some possible considerations in our hypothetical example of the person considering assisted living.

Pros

I will be safer. If I have a fall, someone will be there to help me. (*Do I have complete information about who is on site during the night and who is on call?*)

The place I'm considering has a good reputation. (*How long has it been in business? Is assisted living regulated in this state? If so, what does the public record show?*)

The monthly fee is affordable. (*When was it last raised? Are there any extra charges?*)

I won't be isolated; I'll have a chance to make new friends. (*What is the demographic served by this facility? Are there people in my age group? Are there mostly couples or singles? Men or women?*)

The management offers activities (such as movies, bus trips, a book club) that I can't take advantage of on my own. (*Do they have activities I'm really interested in, things I would do if I weren't living there? Are they affordable?*)

Meals are an option, so I won't have to cook for myself. (*Get some sample menus, and if possible visit during mealtime. What provisions are made for special diets? How rigid are the meal times?*)

I can cook for myself if I don't want to join the meal plan. (*What is the nature of the kitchen facilities in a typical apartment? Some have only microwaves instead of stoves. Are there grocery stores nearby? Do they deliver?*)

Housekeeping and other services are available, so that I no longer have to deal with finding and paying reliable people. (*What services are included? Which ones involve an extra charge?*)

If my condition deteriorates so that I need skilled nursing care, the facility offers that option. (*Is it on the same campus? Nursing homes are regulated in all states; what does the public record show?*)

Cons

If I don't like it, or it becomes unaffordable, I've sold my house (or given up my rent-stabilized apartment). (*Where can I live?*)

It can't be reached by public transportation, which may deter my friends from visiting. (*This happened to a friend of mine, who spent the last few years of her life in an excellent facility that was very difficult to reach—a serious consideration in New York City, where people rely on public transportation.*)

If I want to cook for myself, it may be hard to shop for groceries.

The management wants a lot of personal financial information, to be sure that I won't stop paying.

If I have a fall, the facility might order an ambulance to take me to a hospital for X-rays, which might not be covered by insurance. (*That happened to my mother, and I received a bill for $900 that was not covered by Medicare.*)

There are no religious services on site or there are religious services of the sponsoring institution but not my religion. (*One well-regarded institution in my area serves meals to all residents in accordance with Jewish dietary laws and brings in outside clergy to offer Catholic Mass once a month and Protestant Bible study once a week. Another facility has a Catholic chapel and regular Masses but has often received low scores on other important criteria.*)

There are obviously many other possibilities in any individual situation. How to weigh them? For me, the first con in my hypothetical example would outweigh all the pros. But someone who had other options might give it much less weight. The challenges involved in evaluating the various considerations illustrate the significance of praying for the grace to be in equilibrium. It's important to allow enough time to assess how much weight to assign to each consideration.

5. **Offer the decision to God in prayer.** When a decision has been thoughtfully and unselfishly made, this step may lead to a feeling of peace, a sense of having heard God's call and responded. Thank God for the grace!

No decision is free of risk. An awareness of the risks that are being assumed doesn't necessarily mean the choice was wrong. However, if at this stage there are strong negative emotions, feelings of anxiety out of proportion to the risks involved, it may well mean that the choice was not properly made. Pray for the grace to discern what went wrong. Review the various steps: Were you really in equilibrium? Did you have all the information necessary for an informed choice? Was there an important consideration that you left out? Were you influenced by someone's well-intentioned advice? Have you given too much (or too little) emphasis to the risks?

These are hard questions. Keep asking, What is drawing me to God, and what is drawing me away?

19

Mantras

When my ninety-five-year-old aunt was dying of cancer, she complained that she wasn't able to pray: "Sometimes all I can say to the Lord is 'please' and 'thank you.'" I told her I was pretty sure that was enough.

That kind of experience isn't limited to the terminally ill—as anyone who has suffered a serious injury or major surgery can attest. The loss of someone we love can be at least as overwhelming. The fact is, it's really hard to pray when we're sick or grieving. In these situations, a short phrase or invocation can give comfort when the mind can't focus on a longer prayer. Repetition, aloud or mentally, can have a calming effect, which will be familiar to anyone who has ever practiced centering prayer. I found the Jesus prayer, with its accompanying rhythmic breathing, a particular comfort when I was undergoing an MRI.

This is real prayer, when something requiring more attention is impossible. Here are a few suggestions:

God, come to my assistance; LORD, make haste to
help me.

My grace is sufficient for you. (2 Corinthians 12:9)

I will bless the LORD at all times; his praise shall be always
in my mouth. (Psalm 34:2)

The LORD is my light and my salvation; whom should I
fear? (Psalm 27:1)

Praise the LORD, for he is good, for his mercy endures
forever. (Psalm 136:1)

My help comes from the LORD, the maker of heaven and
earth. (Psalm 121:2)

Do not let your hearts be troubled or afraid. (John 14:27)

The Jesus prayer: Lord Jesus Christ, Son of the Living
God, have mercy on me, a sinner. Or the short version:
Lord Jesus Christ, have mercy on me.

Be still and know that I am God.
Be still and know that I am.
Be still and know.
Be still.
Be.

For all that has been, thank you. For all that is to
        come: yes!

—Dag Hammarskjöld

Let nothing disturb you
Let nothing affright you
All passes away
God only shall stay
Patience wins all
Who has God lacks nothing
For God is his all.

—St. Teresa of Ávila

Please.

Thank you.

Alleluia.

Epilogue: Prayer of a Disciple in Pain

Lord, Jesus, help me remember that I am always in your
    presence.
Hear the Holy Spirit praying within me, and grant me what
    I need.
Grant me the gift of patience.
Teach me to let go of all anxiety and all irrational fear.
Grant me the grace to let go of anger and all negative feelings.
Help me accept dependence, isolation, solitude, sadness, or
    grief as part of the spiritual journey.
Grant me the grace to take up my cross each day and seek help
    when I need it.
Help me to quiet all the internal background noise; to be more
    compassionate, more trusting, and more grateful
and to look forward with hope to eternal life.

Resources

Fleming, David. *What Is Ignatian Spirituality?* Chicago: Loyola Press, 2008.

Harter, Michael, ed. *Hearts on Fire: Praying with Jesuits.* Chicago: Loyola Press, 1993.

Martin, James. *Jesus: A Pilgrimage.* New York: HarperCollins, 2014.

Martin, James. *Learning to Pray: A Guide for Everyone.* New York: HarperCollins, 2021.

Merton, Thomas. *Praying the Psalms.* Collegeville, MN: Liturgical Press, 1956.

About the Author

Barbara Lee is a practicing spiritual director who lives in New York City. She is a retired attorney, a former U.S. magistrate judge, and a long-serving member of the Ignatian Volunteer Corps—an organization of retired people inspired by Ignatian spirituality who perform volunteer work among the poor.

More Books by Barbara Lee

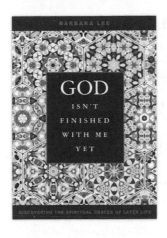

GOD ISN'T FINISHED WITH ME YET

God Isn't Finished with Me Yet shows readers how God meets us with unexpected grace. In five succinct chapters, Barbara Lee shows how Ignatian prayer and discernment offer those later in life a path to discovering previously unknown vocations and new ways of living and being of service.

PB | 978-0-8294-4661-6 | $12.95

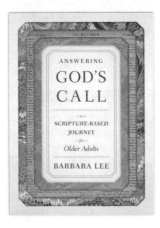

ANSWERING GOD'S CALL

In *Answering God's Call*, spiritual director Barbara Lee uses Scripture-focused prayer to help readers connect with some of our elder saints and consider what God reveals to us through their lives. They demonstrate that true callings are discerned not simply by reason and circumstance, but also through self-knowledge and conversation with God.

PB | 978-0-8294-5131-3 | $12.99

More Ignatian Spirituality Books

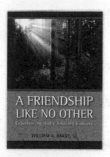

A FRIENDSHIP LIKE NO OTHER

Explore the path to becoming a friend of God. Grounded in biblical tradition and Ignatian spirituality, *A Friendship Like No Other* offers a fresh approach to becoming a friend of God and understanding this relationship.

PB | 978-0-8294-2702-8 | $14.95

A SIMPLE, LIFE-CHANGING PRAYER

In *A Simple, Life-Changing Prayer*, Jim Manney introduces Christians to a 500-year-old form of prayer that dramatically altered his perception of prayer and the way he prayed. The prayer is the examen, which St. Ignatius Loyola developed for the purpose of nurturing a reflective habit of mind that is constantly attuned to God's presence.

PB | 978-0-8294-3535-1 | $9.95

THE IGNATIAN GUIDE TO FORGIVENESS

In *The Ignatian Guide to Forgiveness*, Marina McCoy delves into the principles of Ignatian spirituality and uses gentle honesty to lay out 10 steps toward forgiveness. Each chapter offers stories, real-life steps to take, and a powerful prayer for healing.

PB | 978-0-8294-5007-1 | $13.99

More Ignatian Spirituality Books

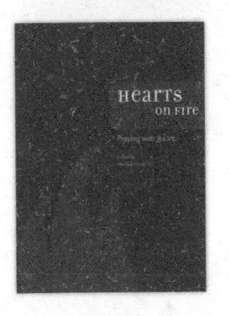